THIS BOOK BELONGS TO:

_____

_____

_____

mantra

For the children of Richard Cobden Primary School, London
D.M.

Special thanks to Phillip Fong and his family,
and to the staff and children of Mason Avenue Kindergarten
J.C.

First published 2003 by Mantra
5 Alexandra Grove, London N12 8NU
www.mantralingua.com

Text copyright © 2003 David Mills
Illustrations copyright © 2003 Julia Crouth
Dual language copyright © 2003 Mantra

British Library Cataloguing in Publication Data:
a catalogue record for this book is available
from the British Library.

El diente flojo, flojito, flojote
The Wibbly Wobbly Tooth

Written by David Mills
Illustrated by Julia Crouth

Spanish translation by Maria Helena Thomas

mantra

El lunes por la noche, a dos minutos para las siete,
Li sintió su primer diente flojo.
El diente estaba flojo, flojito, flojote.

On Monday evening at two minutes past seven, Li got his first wobbly tooth.
And the tooth went...Wibble Wobble

El martes se lo enseñó a todo el mundo en el colegio...
El diente estaba flojo, flojito, flojote.

On Tuesday, he had to show everyone at school.
And the tooth went...Wibble Wobble.

El miércoles tuvo que tener mucho cuidado mientras almorzaba...
El diente estaba flojo, flojito, flojote.

On Wednesday, he had to be careful eating his lunch.
And the tooth went...Wibble Wobble, Wibble Wobble.

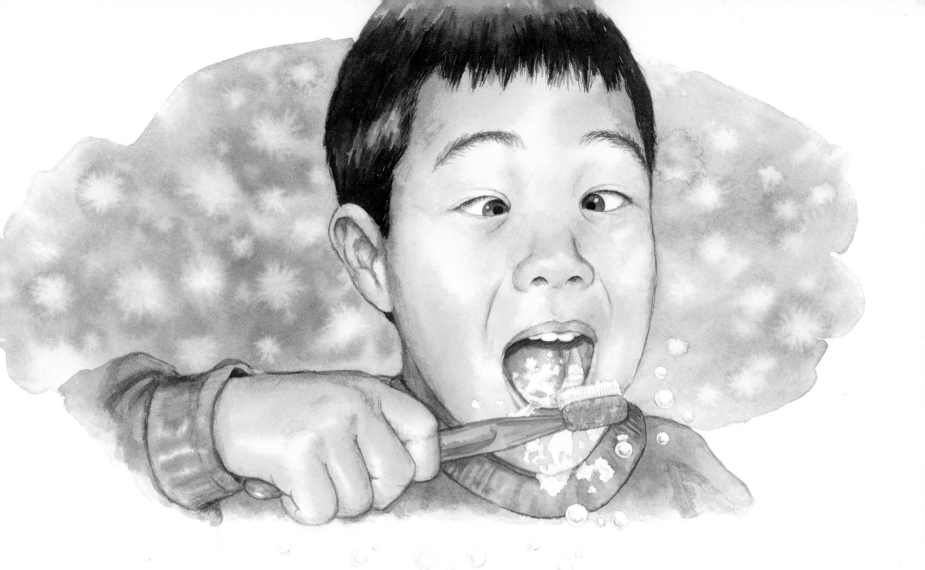

El jueves Li tuvo que tener mucho cuidado mientras se cepillaba los dientes...
El diente estaba flojo, flojito, flojote.

On Thursday, Li had to be extremely careful brushing his teeth.
And the tooth went...Wibble Wobble, Wibble Wobble, Wibble.

El viernes Li se aflojaba el diente cada vez más...

On Friday, Li wiggled his tooth in and out,

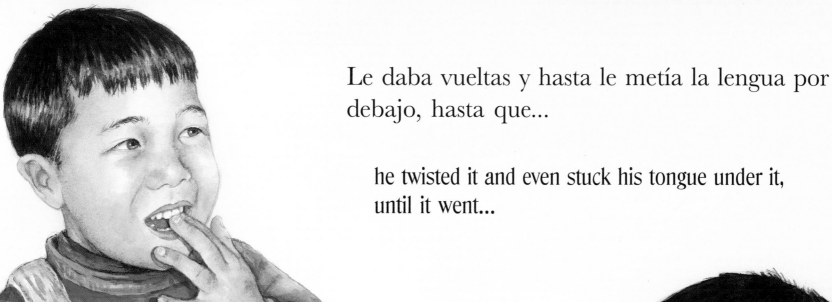

Le daba vueltas y hasta le metía la lengua por debajo, hasta que...

he twisted it and even stuck his tongue under it, until it went...

FLOJO, FLOJITO,
FLOJOTE

¡Ups!

WIBBLE WOBBLE, WIBBLE
WOBBLE,
WIBBLE WOBBLE...

OOOOPS!

"HURRAY!" everyone cheered.
Li gave them a big smile and he felt very brave.

"¡HURRA!" -dijeron todos.
Li sonrió ampliamente y se sintió muy valiente.

Cuando llegó la hora de irse a casa, Li salió corriendo para enseñarle el diente a su papá.

When it was time to go home, Li rushed out to show his dad.

"Por fin." -dijo el papá - "¡Muy bien!"

"At last," said Dad. "Well done!"

El sábado Li echó de menos su diente.
Quería que le saliera uno nuevo.

On Saturday, Li missed his front tooth.
He really wanted a new tooth.

"Ven," -dijo papá, -"vamos a casa de la abuela. Ella sabrá qué hacer."
Y se fueron a casa de la abuela.

"Come on," said Dad. "Let's go and see Grandma. She'll know just what to do."
So off they went to Grandma's.

¡Mira!" -dijo Li.

"¡Se te ha caído un diente!" -dijo Joey. "¡Si lo pones debajo de la almohada vendrá un hada y te dará dinero por él!"

"¿Por qué?" -preguntó Li.

"¡Porque necesita tu diente para construir su nueva casa!"

"¡Ah!" -dijo Li. "Mejor se lo digo a mi abuela."

"Look!" said Li.

"Hey, you've lost your tooth!" said Joey.

"If you put it under the pillow, the tooth fairy will come and bring you some money!"

"Why?" asked Li.

"She needs your tooth to build her new house!"

"Oh," said Li. "I'd better tell my Grandma!"

"¡Mira!" -dijo Li.
"¡Oh!" -dijo Kofi -"¡Yo enterré el mío y me creció uno nuevo!"
"¿De verdad? ¡Tendré que contárselo a mi abuela!"

"Look!" said Li.
"Oooooo!" said Kofi. "I hid mine in the ground and then my new one grew!"
"Did it really? I must tell my Grandma!"

"¡Mira!" -dijo Li.

"¡Anda!" -dijo Salma. "¡Si lo echas al río te traerá buena suerte!"

"¿Seguro? -preguntó Li. "¿Qué hago, papá?"

"La abuela sabrá." -respondió el papá.

"Look!" said Li.

"Hey," said Salma. "You could throw your tooth into the river and it will bring you good luck!"

"It will?" said Li. "Dad, what shall I do?"

"Grandma knows," said Dad.

"¡Abuela, abuela, MIRA!" -dijo Li -"¡Mi diente estaba
FLOJO, FLOJITO, FLOJOTE, FLOJO, FLOJITO,
FLOJOTE y FUERA!"
"Bien." -dijo la abuela sonriendo- "¡Yo sé exactamente
lo que hay que hacer! Échalo sobre el techo del vecino
y pide un deseo muy grande." -le susurró la abuela.
"OKAY" -gritó Li y...

"Grandma, grandma, LOOK!" said Li. "My tooth went WIBBLE WOBBLE
WIBBLE WOBBLE WIBBLE WOBBLE and OUT!"
"Well, well, well," smiled Grandma. "I know just what to do!" she
whispered. "Throw it up onto a neighbour's roof and make a big wish."
"OK," shouted Li and...

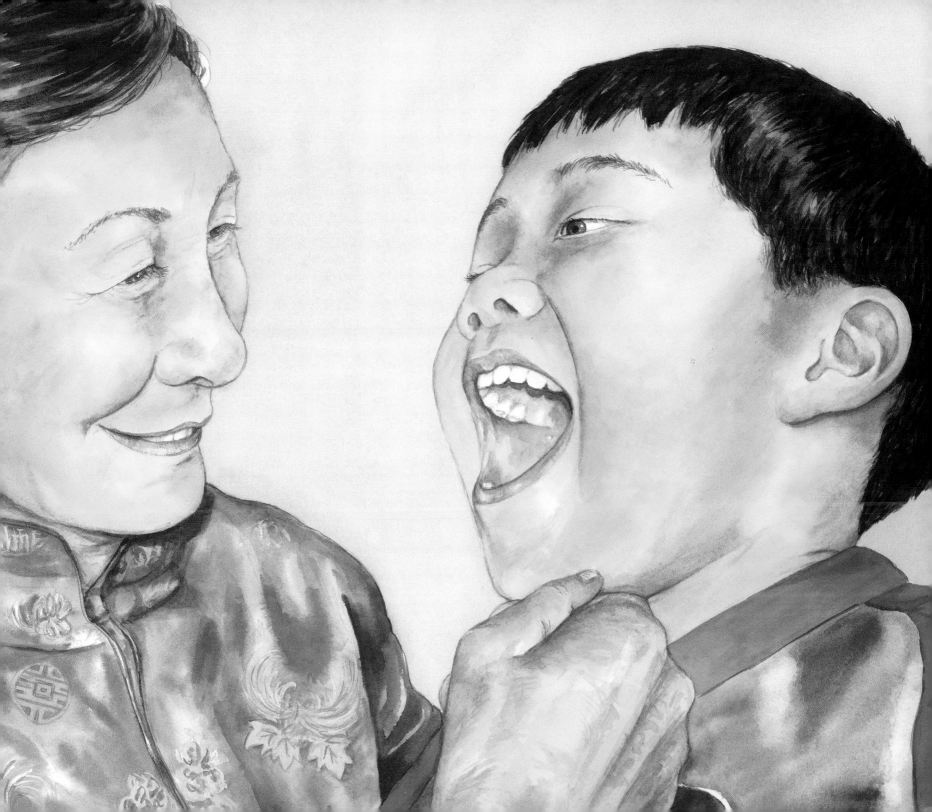

...¡tiró el diente con toda su fuerza!

...threw his tooth up with all his might!

El día siguiente era domingo.
Y no ocurrió nada.

The next day was Sunday.
And nothing happened.

Pero el domingo siguiente, a dos minutos para las siete,
el deseo de Li se convirtió en realidad!

But the next Sunday morning at two minutes past seven, Li's wish came true!

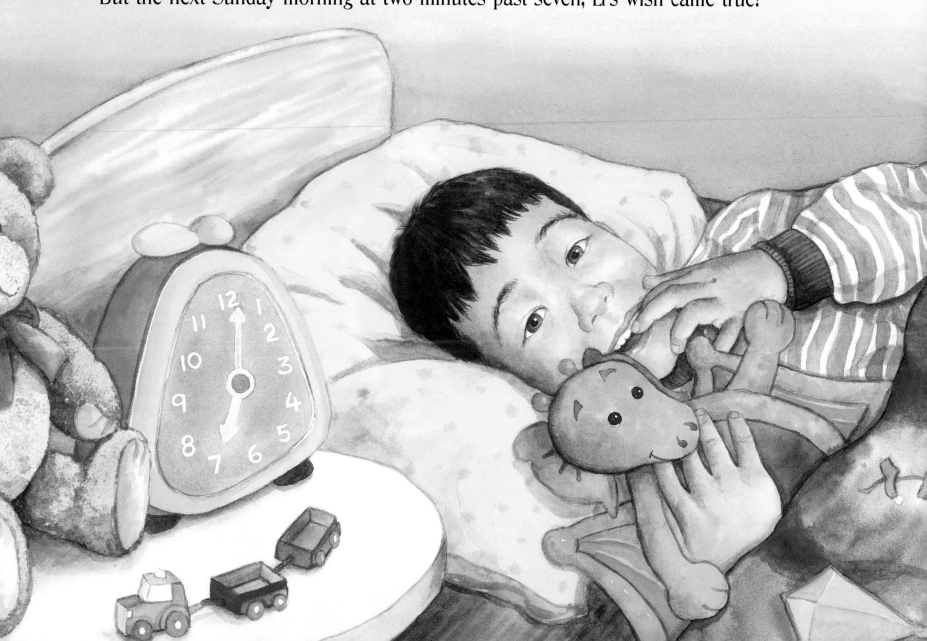

"Mamá, papá," -susurró Li- "¡Miren!"

"Mum, Dad," whispered Li. "Look!"

TOOTHY QUESTIONS

1. Have you lost your first tooth yet?

2. What do we need our teeth for?

3. How do you take care of your teeth?

4. When did you last visit the dentist?

5. Which one of these is best for taking care of teeth?
   a. Eating chocolate
   b. Brushing your teeth twice a day
   c. Climbing a tree

6. In some parts of the world people use different things to clean their teeth. Can you guess which they use?
   a. Apples
   b. Tea leaves
   c. Twigs

7. Which of these animals have the biggest teeth?
   a. Rats
   b. Wolves
   c. Elephants

TOOTHY ANSWERS

2. We need our teeth for eating and talking. They also make us look good when we smile!

5. Brushing your teeth twice a day.

6. Twigs from the Neem tree which grows in South Asia. They fight bacteria, protecting both the teeth and gums. The Neem tree is well known for its medicinal uses.

7. Elephants. Did you know that the tusks of an African elephant can grow up to 3.5 meters!